The Legend Of The Golden Butterfly

The Legend Of The Golden Butterfly

Bruno Egidio Miglietta

La Leggenda Della Farfalla Dorata

English Version

Bruno Egidio Miglietta

This book is Dedicated to:
A special person in my life
He makes all the people that know him.
Part of his life.

Daniel Druehl.

North Fort Myers. Florida.

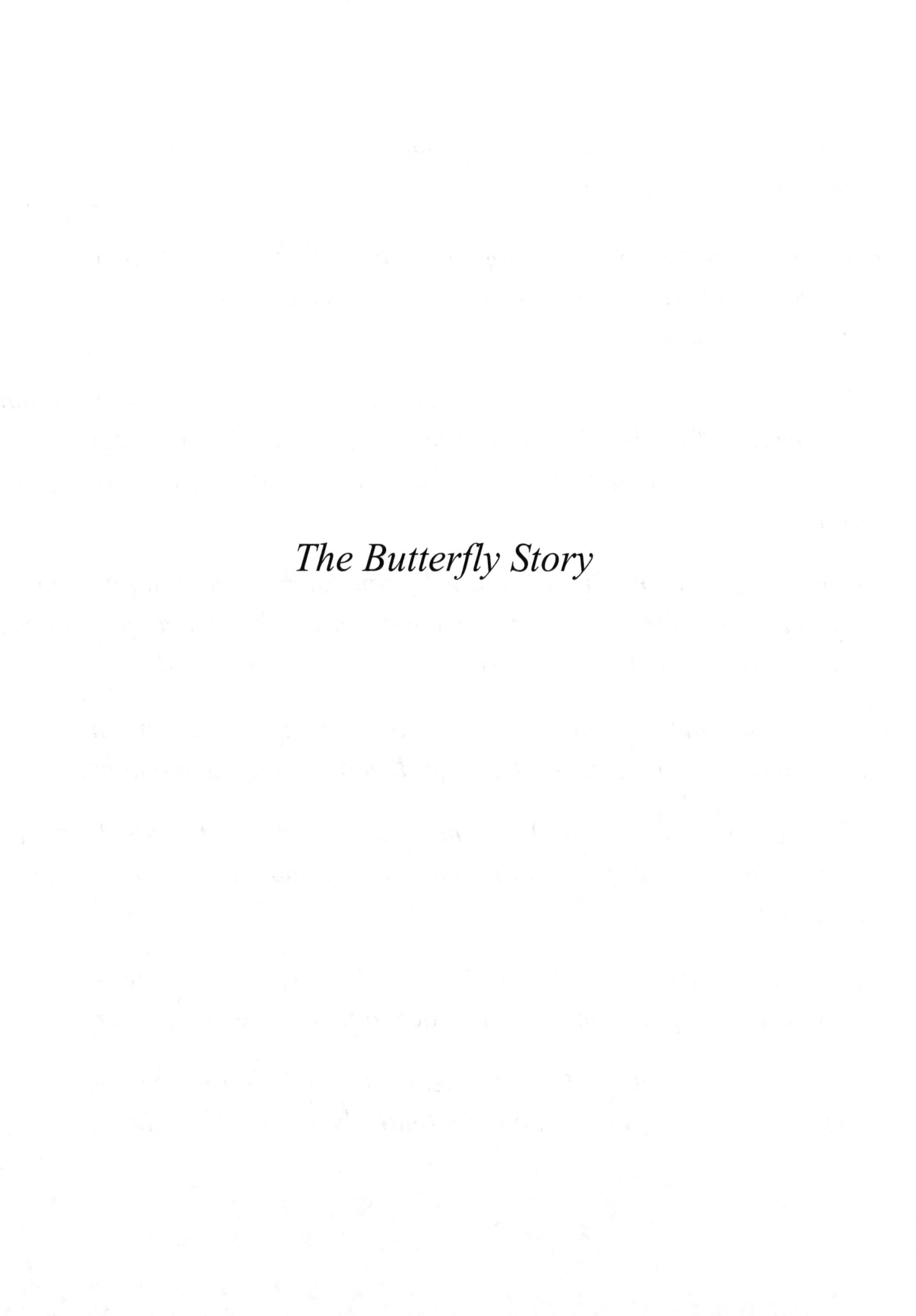

The Butterfly Story

The Legend Of The Golden Butterfly

The Butterfly Story

Millions of Butterflies gather together in the forest, every year, for a special event, which no one can explain.

The place where this story happens is in the Chu Cerchuk Forest. The vegetation does not grow there, the butterfly shapes can be seen only from the sky.

The gathering of the millions of butterflies in the forest is an annual celebration. They immigrate to a burning ground in formation, where they will stay for several days. They make the shape of one giant Butterfly.

Some people say that it's the butterfly sanctuary; others say it's the perfect habitat for the butterfly. No one knows why this happens and with the years maybe for curiosity it has become a legend.

But.... Someone has said that it's not a legend is a true story and an unknown author has written a book about the golden butterfly.

Who has this book? A monkey, whose name is Virco. He has the book that his great, great grandfather has written and claims that it's the true story.

I am a naturalist researcher and I have the curiosity to know why these events happen, only in this place, and how this event starts.

Virco lives in a nature reserve. I decide to see him. I have asked him to tell me the story about the giant butterfly and his Grandfather.

The Legend Of The Golden Butterfly

The Butterfly Story

Virco agrees to tell me the story, but he says. "Remember…nothing means nothing."

This means a lot of bananas for him. And it is okay by me. He sits on one of the top branches of a small Banacua tree, opens his book. I sit on the ground.

Virco starts the story by saying that his great Grandfather. Goco is trying to rest on the top of a tree, when he sees Gokor, The Master Spider Monkey who says, "Come down Goco. I have a job for you."

"Grandfather comes down from the tree to meet the Master Spider Monkey and responds, "A job for me? I have a job already Master Monkey; I rest and catch the sun."

The Master Monkey Gokor says, "Goco." This job is very important."

Grandfather askes, "What kind of a job is it, to be so important?"

The Master Monkey says. "Come with me and you will see."

"Oh I come, I follow you Master don't worry. I follow you print steps. After one hour walking Goco says, "Master we are lost?"

"No Goco, we are not lost; we go to a very special place." responds the Master Monkey and we go in the right direction."

"A okay I follow you." Grandfather says.

The Master Monkey stops in front of a Machacurker tree and says to Grandfather, "Goco, clean your feet you are in a sacred land."

The Legend Of The Golden Butterfly

The Butterfly Story

Grandfather looks on the ground, scratches his head and says, "Sacred ground? Look all the same to me but if you say that is sacred it's okay to me. I clean my feet."
With two leaves he cleans the bottom of is feet and the Master Monkey says, "Now you follow me." and he leads Grandfather to a small tree.

The Master Monkey said, "Goco. Look at the top of this leaf and you will see a golden egg. This is a special egg. Your job will be here to stay, day and night, and watch the egg. If you see any change you will come and let me know."

Grandfather does not know what to do, or what to think. He thinks he has a job watching one egg. He says. "This is an easy job."

Then the Master Monkey says. "You need to write everything that happens day by day, about this egg."

"Write everything?" Askes Grandfather.

"Oh yes. Everything" Responds the Master Monkey. "Start now."

"A okay" says Grandfather. "I sit over here and I watch, I have my bananas to eat."

For many days Grandfather, did not move from watching the egg. He sleeps with one eye open and for those days the egg did nothing. On day six the egg started to move, Grandfather noticed that on the leaves were two eggs and the next day there were three eggs and the leaves on the tree had disappeared.

The Legend Of The Golden Butterfly

The Butterfly Story

Grandfather asked himself. "What has happed to the leaves? I must go and see the supreme monkey."

He walks deep inside the forest.
When he gets to the Master Monkey he says, "Goco your presence is good news. What is the news you deliver to me today?"

Grandfather responds, "Yesterday there were two eggs, today there are three eggs, and the leaves on the tree have disappeared."

"Good sign, very good said the Master Monkey. The egg is now a small caterpillar. You will follow everywhere it goes, and you will measure it every day."

"I need to measure?" Grandfather responds, "With what?"

"With your foot and your tail." Master Monkey says.

"All right." responds Grandfather. "I will do it today but I can tell you that the egg… no, the thee eggs, are small like my foot. Okay… I need to write everything in the book, I go home."

Grandfather, on his way back, sees that the caterpillar was bigger and moved from branch to branch. It eats all the leaves on the tree and moves to another tree.

"Today I will need to write." said Grandfather.
"Today is a very sunny day; the caterpillar is seven days old and one of my monkey foot long."
Grandfather was tired he says, "I will watch every day. And I write two times a week. I need to sleep."

~4~

The Legend Of The Golden Butterfly

The Butterfly Story

The caterpillar grows day by day; it eats all the leafs from tree to tree, and starts to eat the leafs on the ground.

"Wow." Says Grandfather, "You never stop eating. You are so fat and big, you better take it easy okay, you can get a big indigestion. And I am not a doctor."

Then Grandfather has to think, after he has is thinking says to the caterpillar. "You need to explain to me how I can measure you, if you move, and eat all the time, you better take a break this way I can measure you, do you understand me? If I ask you why I have this job you don't know, but I know that you are a big problem for me, only this I know. Okay, okay I will bring more leafs to you."

Someday go by, the Master Monkey comes to see grand father and to see the caterpillar. Master Monkey says. "I see the caterpillar is big very big however, it is not big enough."

Grandfather responds, "It is not big enough? She ate the leafs of the tree over a square mile, I walk every day all day, and I don't have ~5~ shoes on my feet Master Monkey."

Master Monkey says, "Goco she needs to eat more and you need to be ready for your job coming very soon. Remember she needs to eat all the time."

Grandfather responds, "She better start eating the trunks."

"Ho no." said the Master Monkey. "You need to bring the leafs to her this is your job."

The Butterfly Story

"What?" Said grandfather, "Bring leafs to her?"

"Yes and remember." Said the Master Monkey. "The more she grows the more she eats. I will come to see her in one week."

The follows days the caterpillar eats very slowly but she moves very fast. For many days Grandfather goes to the top of the tree and throws down the leafs to the caterpillar that follows him from tree to tree.

Now Grandfather, has a big, big problem, how he can measure the caterpillar, she has grown to be twenty-one monkey feet long and growing fast every day. She moves very slow and makes funny sounds. She has changes color from green to yellow, that's okay? but? How he can measure the height?
He started to think about it and the caterpillar pushes him from the back. "Now this I don't like." says Grandfather.

"I was thinking okay?... And stop making this noise I have headache and I have hard time thinking okay? The Master Monkey has all the answers about you, he comes tomorrow..."

The Butterfly Story

The Master Monkey did not come back to see the caterpillar as he promised. It was a rainy day; Grandfather went to see him in the forest. The Master Monkey was on top of a tree, to see Grandfather asked, "Goco what news you bring me today? The fall comes very soon and the gold cocoon is not big enough."

Grandfather said. "She is so big she does not move fast anymore and she is making strange sound. I carry leafs every day for her and I am tired I need help."

"She is hungry and she needs more food, said the Master Monkey. Find a banana leaf to help you to bring leafs to the caterpillar."

Grandfather asked the Master Monkey. "Why he was the only one chosen for this big job."

"You have lots of patience." said the Master Monkey.

Grandfather responds, "I do not have patience anymore I have lost all my patience and I do not know where."

The Master Monkey says. "She needs to eat."

"I know." Responds Grandfather, "I need to measure and write the book every day and to bring leafs to her. She is hungry all the time, now I go home Master."

"Remember." Said Master Monkey, "Someday, you will be the monkey that everyone will remember. They will remember you by your name."

The Butterfly Story

"Oh yes responds Grandfather, "To be the monkey that watches one gold egg. I come to see you again Master Monkey, I have a job to do to find her, goodbye."

Grandfather to go back home he gets lost he takes a different paths and he found a banana tree he took one leaf. He looked around and saw many banana trees he started to picks up leafs to bring to the caterpillar.

Grandfather finds that he is going a long way for the banana leafs and the caterpillar is growing at the rate of one monkey tail a day.
The caterpillar likes the banana leafs and Grandfather thinks it would be a good idea to bring her closer to the banana field. It would be so much easier for him. It will be less work.

He says to the caterpillar, "You cannot move anymore. I will need help moving you. I go and see Mr. Owl and I asked him to help me.
He knows everything. He sleeps all day; he will be okay if I wake him for a small question. You stay here; I will come back for you."

He goes to see Mr. Owl. On the tree was a sign, it says, "I stay awake all night, and I sleep during the day. Please do not disturb me… go away." Grandfather calls Mister Owl a few times he opens the door and asks Grandfather, "Do you not see what the sign says. What is it you want? I hope it is very important to wake me up so early."

Grandfather responds, "I have a caterpillar that is two hundred fifty monkey feet long, and it needs to be moved. I need your help please."

The Butterfly Story

Mister. Owl says, "Hummm that is a big move a caterpillar. There is only one company that is good for that job. How you end up with this job Goco."

Grandfather responds, "I don't know."

Mister Owl says, "The Ants, Co. I recommend them. Go where the water fall is, and you will find them."

Grandfather responds, "Thank you, Mr. Owl. I will go into the forest to find the Ant, Co."

Grandfather starts walking and thinking. "But there are many water falls into the forest. How can I choose the waterfall where the. Ant, Co. is. I will follow the river."

He finds the Ant. Co. office next to the Ouk Barqu waterfall. There were a big signs on the wall saying, "We move everything. Complete service. No job is too big or too small."

An ant comes into the office, and asked grandfather if he needs help, Grandfather says, "Yes, my name is Goco. Can you move a giant caterpillar?"

The ant answers. "Yes, we can move the caterpillar, we charge by the length, the height, and weight, my name is Antete and I am the group leader of this company the Ant. Co. professional movers, we will come to measure the caterpillar tomorrow."

"Ho, no? Responds Grandfather you come today it is an emergency."

The Butterfly Story

Antete says, "Okay priority one job, we can do the job today, we never say no to the customer, then Antete asked Grandfather, "How will you pay for it?"

"Pay?..." Says Grandfather, "Nobody paid me to watch her."

Antete said, "Nothing means nothing. Do you understand friend? We can come up with one solution. We come to see the caterpillar. If we move her, when she leaves the cocoon, we will take the cocoon, in payment is that ok with you."

Grandfather responds, "I don't understand what that means. She lives in the cocoon, who?"

"Ho, you do not know." Antete says, "I explain to you. The caterpillar is an egg and when it is ready and full grown, who lives inside needs to come out; it cannot use the cocoon anymore but? We can use it. Okay?"

Grandfather said. "It's a deal."

Antete asked, "Where is the caterpillar?"

"Next to the river." Said Grandfather and, "She needs to be moved to the banana field."

Antete pulls out a big map jump on the forest map and with a big lens he sees the caterpillar location, the banana fields, and says, "Hummm... It is a long move with a lot of room to turn right and left, the ground is flat that is good, is dry field that is good, lots of shade that is good, in one hour we do the job.

The Legend Of The Golden Butterfly

The Butterfly Story

Mister you are okay. The Ant, Co. it's on your service day and night, we do the job, and we do not ask why."

Grandfather asks, "For curiosity I need to ask and if a tree his in the way, what will happen?... You don't move the caterpillar?"

Antete responds, "Oh no we move the caterpillar it's not a problem but if we have too many trees and we need more room, we will need the beavers company to help us. Mr. Beaver will cat down the trees for us. We use Mr. Beaver service only for emergency."

My Grandfather asked, "How will you move her?
I do not want her to be hurt."

"Oh sentimental feeling I understand, don't worry. We will lift her very, very, gently.
She doesn't feel that we move her. Antete said, "To do a good job is priority one for our company. We are professionals; we have six groups of movers in our company, climbing, flat walking, dawn carrying, push, and lift."

Antete walks outside his office, whistles and thousands of ants appear, he says, "We have a big job to do, all be ready and please no one call in sick." He enters his office and says to my grandfather, "Now we will need your signature and we will follow you."
Grandfather signed his name and the ants followed him to where the big caterpillar was. When they saw the caterpillar Antete said, "This is a big job, everyone takes a moment of silence butt a deep breath. No job is too big or too small, don't be scared by the size of the job, be scare to don't do the job, company ready...let's go."

The Legend Of The Golden Butterfly

The Butterfly Story

The ants line up in formation to move the caterpillar. When everyone takes is position the back group says, "Ant we are ready," The center group, says, "We are ready to." The front group says, "We are waiting for you."

When the entire group was ready Antete says, "Okay…stop talking I know will have a big cocoon, we can use as boat to take a cruise around the world now communication please, now lift and let's go."

They lifted the caterpillar and they ran without stopping for one hour to complete their job.

As soon as they put the caterpillar down, she began to eat the banana leafs. "We will come back for the cocoon." Says Antete.

"Ok." said Grandfather he watches the caterpillar eating.
When he was dark he prepared a bed on the top of the tree and he fell asleep. When he woke up in the morning, he was surprised because he did not see the caterpillar. He looked around and saw her long tracks toward the lake. Grandfather was mad saying, "I cannot believe, she cannot walk to eat but she can walk to watch the view.
Where is she now?"

When he looked down the lake, he sees the caterpillar inside the lake…

Grandfather has written that the caterpillar was bigger than before, the forest trees look small in comparison to her size.
Now Grandfather does not know what to do, how to get her out of the lake. He was thinking, "I call back the Ant Co. again. I need to talk to that caterpillar now, and she better listen to me."

The Legend Of The Golden Butterfly

The Butterfly Story

Grandfather was very upset, he goes to face the caterpillar, and says, "You need to stop leaving and disappearing. I do not know what to do any more to feed you, stay in one place please."

Then he sees a water fall that spills in to a big river and into a large lake. Grandfather thinks, "If I throw leafs into the river, the river will carry them into the lake, and then she can eat and drink."

Grandfather follows the river he climbs on the top of the tree and start throwing leafs into the river. He sleeps few hours a day on the tree and works long hours each day gathering leafs.

One day in the morning Grandfather decides to go down to the lake to see the caterpillar he sees that leafs are in the river, "Oh no...and now what append?" Said Grandfather he hears the caterpillar and decides to go check on her. When he reaches the lake, he was surprised to find that the lake is dry. He thinks the caterpillar drank all the water then he notices that there are no leafs at the bottom of the lake.

The caterpillar is making a lot of noise and Grandfather thinks, "She is hungry."

His thoughts are, "I have only two hands. You are one in three. You drink a lot, you eat a lot, and you complain a lot, and you are a big problem to me, and I am right."

Grandfather follows the river until he comes to a big fallen tree across the river and leafs are getting caught in the branches of the tree acting as a dam and causing the river to change direction.

The Legend Of The Golden Butterfly

The Butterfly Story

This creates a big swamp. He sees a Beaver and he says to the Beaver, "Now tell me. Did you do this?"

"No." said the Beaver. I did not do anything wrong okay? I sharpen my teeth on the tree and it falls dawn."

Grandfather says, "You Beaver cut this tree and stopped the water in the river from going into the lake. I have a big caterpillar to feed. Call for help to clear up this mess."

The Beaver whistles and seven Beavers come out running from the woods.
They started to cut the tree in pieces, clean up the branches and the water started to go back into the lake.

The beaver looks up on the hill and says, "Too much water is going into the river, everybody run."

The river became very big Grandfather and the Beaver were caught by the flowing water, they were carried down river but then were able to grab a tree branch. They were saved and able to walks in the woods.

Then Grandfather saw the water current push the caterpillar out of the lake. Grandfather says, "I must go after her."

The beaver responds, "No, no, it is not safe, for you to go there. The river is still dangerous. If you must go, go through the woods and go around the lake."

Grandfather runs into the woods went around the lake but could not find the caterpillar. Then he heard the trees breaking.

The Legend Of The Golden Butterfly

The Butterfly Story

He saw the caterpillar moving toward him says, "I do not expect this. She looks like a big green submarine on land."

Then he saw many birds flying south, and the animals running. They are leaving the forest, he says to himself, "I think this is strange where they all are going? There is no fire in the forest, I don't smell smoke?"

So, he asked, "Where is everyone going?"

A deer answered, "We are all going south, because the cold from the north is coming this way."

Grandfather says, "We are in the south."

A water buffalo responds, "We mean further south, friend."

Grandfather hears "Goco, you are doing a very good job."
He sees the Master, Grand Master Spider Monkey, with the Master Monkey. I come a long way said the Master, Grand Master Spider Monkey to see this beautiful cocoon and thanks to you, Goco she will be ready in a couple of days."

Grandfather was confuse and asked the Grand Master Spider Monkey, "She will be ready? Ready for what?"

"To fly." The Grand Master Spider Monkey responds.

"Fly?" Says Grandfather.

"Yes fly." Responds, the Grand Master Spider Monkey, and you can go with her. If do you want to go."

The Butterfly Story

"Ho no…?" Says Grandfather, "The highest, I can go is on the top of the tree I don't fly."

"The caterpillar pushed Grandfather from the back and Grandfather says to the caterpillar, "I am not finished with you, yet."

"She knows you very well, responds the Grand Master Spider Monkey. You helped her to survive, her job is to fly north and save millions of butterfly's."

My grandfather asked, "What is she?"

"She is a giant golden butterfly and she will never forget you." Responds, the Master Monkey.

Grandfather asked, "Is my job finished?"

The Master Grand Master Monkey says, "When she turns in to a gold butterfly, your job is finished, yes."

The Caterpillar turned and went in to the woods, grandfather ask, "Where are you going now? I am tired of following you around."

"Let her go Goco but stay close to her, we go now we can watch her from the top of the mountain flying when she is ready." The Master Grand Master Monkey says.

"A okay grandfather responds I follow her."
The caterpillar never stops walking; Grandfather was too tired to follow her and says, "When you go north? I will go south.

The Legend Of The Golden Butterfly

The Butterfly Story

I will go to the beach; I will find a tree, build a bed, and go to sleep. You can walk all you want; do not get in trouble."

"Grandfather finds a sha she ku tree on the beach. He makes the bed and falls asleep; he was awakened by a loud noise. He opens his eyes and was surprised to find the caterpillar looking straight at him, face to face.

"He says what the matter with you? You scare me this way; you are supposed to go north, you have something to do. Go and Goodbye."

Grandfather looks at the caterpillar and says, "I do not want you to go but if you go I will wait for you, you are now my friend."

The caterpillar went in to the forest; hours go by the caterpillar does not return, grandfather starts to worry. He went to the top of the tree. He did not see the caterpillar for all day. Grandfather starts to worry more; he looks for tracks, and asks himself, where can she be? If she turns into a butterfly the cocoon shell needs to be nearby.

He did not see tracks leading to where she is so; he went back on the beach. As he was looking, from the beach, he saw the cocoon was far away on the top of the water. He also saw what looked like a giant bird flying, he was looking in the direction of the sun and it was too bright and shiny with the sun light to see clear what it was.

As it comes closer he saw that it was a gold giant butterfly, she landed on the beach near Grandfather. Grandfather says, "You are the most beautiful butterfly I have ever seen."

The Legend Of The Golden Butterfly

The Butterfly Story

The butterfly opened her wing and my Grandfather says, "You want me to come with you?" He got on the butterfly and they flew over the forest all day then landed on the beach.
"Grandfather says, "Go. Do what you have to do. I will wait for you to come back."

The butterfly gently moves her head and Grandfather sees the butterfly move her wings. She flies high into the sky. Grandfather needs to wait for the butterfly to come back, he misses her.
He watches the sky looking for her.

He waited several weeks; finally Grandfather gave up hope of ever seeing her again. One day it was in the afternoon he saw her flying over the beach with many butterflies under her wings.
He was so happy to see her that he followed her flight which guided him into the forest.
The butterfly landed in the forest. When Grandfather reached her, she was next to the waterfall; he was surrounded by millions of butterflies. Grandfather began crying as he looked at her. The butterfly looks at Grandfather, and she walks to him. She closes her eyes putting her head on his chest. Grandfather says, "I am waiting for you. You are tired you need rest. I will take care of you. You are my best friend."
They spend lots of time together flying all over the forest.
Grandfather doesn't write anymore."

"This is the story of a metamorphosis of the Golden Butterfly."

The End.

The Legend Of The Golden Butterfly

Book For Children

Augustine The Ghost Of August
Crunch, Crunch, Crunch, In The Woods
Donky The Donkey
Tasso The Painting Mouse
The Carousel Horse
The Ringing Bell
The Moose With The Christmas Spirit
I Touched The Moon
Pegasus The Black Stallion
Where Does Pizza Come From?
Gerard And The Pizza Three
The Lost key
Imbriam Messenger Of God
The Legend Of The Golden Butterfly

The Legend Of The Golden Butterfly

Bruno Egidio Miglietta

Born In Nardò Italy Lives In North Fort Myers FL.